Sheffield

AND ITS REGION

AN HISTORIC CITY

Iron Age beginnings, Norman castles, the Talbots
and the captive queen, ancient buildings

The earliest remnant of settlement in Sheffield is the Iron Age fortification at Wincobank, $2^1/_2$ miles (6km) north-east of the city centre. Probably constructed by the tribe of Brigantes as the Romans approached from the south, fragments of pottery and flint tools have been excavated here. Fine views can be had from the 3 acres (1.2ha) of enclosed hilltop, looking out over the Don Valley towards Sheffield.

•

Around the year 1150 William de Lovetot, a Norman baron, built a wooden castle at the confluence of the Rivers Don and Sheaf; it was around this that the city of Sheffield grew. A larger, stone castle was erected on the same site in 1270 but was demolished after the Civil War in 1648. All we can see today are a few foundations under the Castle Market but the nearby Lady's Bridge over the River Don is a replacement for a structure first built in the 12th century.

The powerful Talbots, Earls of Shrewsbury, became associated with

Sheffield in the Middle Ages. George, the 4th Earl, took up residence at the castle and became one of the most important men in the city's history. In 1516 he built Manor Lodge, a country house more congenial to live in than the castle, on the breezy top of Sheffield Park, 2 miles (5km) to the south-east. His grandson, the 6th Earl, is best remembered as custodian of Mary Queen of Scots in her years of incarceration after she fled to England in 1568. The well-preserved Turret House at Manor Lodge was probably purpose-built to house the captive queen.

Few early buildings remain in Sheffield. The half-timbered Old Queen's Head, first documented in 1582, stands in Pond Hill. The cathedral, on Church Street, was once the parish church of Saints Peter and Paul, but was raised to cathedral status in

LEFT: The Turret House at Manor Lodge was probably built to house Mary Queen of Scots in the 16th century.

RIGHT: The beautiful half-timbered Bishops' House in Meersbrook Park is one of the city's best-loved museums.

FAR RIGHT: The medieval parish church of St Peter and St Paul was raised to cathedral status in 1914.

BELOW: Sheffield from the south-east as engraved by Henry Perlee Parker two centuries ago.

1914. It contains monuments to the 4th and 6th Earls of Shrewsbury in the Shrewsbury Chapel, and the restored Chapel of St George.

The timber-framed Broom Hall, dating from the early 16th century, lies to the north of Ecclesall Road. Some of the best panelled rooms in the city can be seen in the lower Don Valley at Carbrook Hall (1623), now a public house. Paradise Square near the cathedral has many fine red brick Georgian town houses.

Out and About

Wincobank Hill Fort. Iron Age earthworks. Fine views.

Manor Lodge and Turret House. Ruined mansion and restored turret (not presently open to the public but can be viewed from Manor Lane, off City Road).

Old Queen's Head. Half-timbered public house close to the Bus Station.

The cathedral. Adjacent to Church Street, surrounded on three sides by old buildings of several periods.

Broom Hall. Large former rural mansion now in leafy suburbs north of Ecclesall Road (visible from Broomhall Road).

Carbrook Hall. Public house once surrounded by steel works and back-to-back houses in lower Don Valley, now replaced with new manufacturing, retail and office developments.

Paradise Square. Georgian elegance in the old town's heart. Best seen in evenings or Sundays when not filled with parked cars.

FOUNDATIONS OF INDUSTRY

Pioneers of iron, cutlery and silver plate

The happy juxtaposition of iron ore for smelting, oak woods for charcoal and fast flowing streams for water power on Sheffield's western edge gave rise to the metal trades that were later to make the place world famous.

The industrial hamlet in Abbeydale, below Ecclesall Wood, was built in the 18th century to make scythes and small tools. Water wheels drove tilt hammers to forge metal ingots; another drove grinding machinery to put a sharp edge on tools. Of great antiquity is the so-called Shepherd Wheel in Whiteley Woods, referred to in 1584, and in use into the 1930s for sharpening new knives and edge tools.

In the lower Loxley Valley, north-west of Sheffield, is Little Matlock Rolling Mills. Known to have been in operation in the 1790s, it was a water-powered grinding workshop for edge tools but by 1814 had become a tilt forge. Destroyed by the disastrous 'Sheffield Flood' of 1864 (when Bradfield's Dale Dike reservoir burst) it was rebuilt in 1882 as a rolling mill for the manufacture of small steel bars and rods, and is now the only water-powered rolling mill in existence.

ABOVE LEFT: *The 18th-century Abbeydale Industrial Hamlet in the city's south-western suburbs is a fully restored example of Sheffield's pioneering edge-tool industry.*

LEFT: *A fine example of an epergne in Old Sheffield Plate, on display in the City Museum's collection at Weston Park.*

Cutlery manufacture began in Sheffield in the Middle Ages and there were many cutlers recorded here by 1536. The prestigious Company of Cutlers in Hallamshire was founded in 1624. The names of George Wostenholm, Mappin & Webb and Walker & Hall are synonymous with the finest Sheffield-made cutlery.

Sheffield has had its share of inventive genius. Benjamin Huntsman, a clockmaker, in the mid-18th century invented crucible steel. This was a far superior metal to others then available and led to a great expansion of Sheffield's steel industry. Thomas Boulsover, a cutler in the town, invented Sheffield Plate, a method of coating metal objects with a layer of silver which he discovered accidentally! Sheffield became world famous for its silver-plated objects.

ABOVE: *A fantastic example of the Sheffield cutler's art in the City Museum's collection at Weston Park.*

What to See

Abbeydale Industrial Hamlet and Shepherd Wheel. Fine examples of the city's industrial heritage.

The City Museum, Weston Park. Finest collection of Sheffield Plate in the world and a wonderful collection of Sheffield-made cutlery.

The Cutlers' Hall, opposite the cathedral in Church Street, can be viewed by appointment.

Benjamin Huntsman's grave can be seen in the restored grounds of Hill Top Cemetery, Attercliffe Common.

SMOKE, SOOT AND SPARKS

Steel capital of the world

From the middle of the 19th century, Sheffield grew rapidly into the world's foremost steel manufacturing centre. The industry was based on the level ground of the lower Don Valley east of the heart of the town. Enterprising individuals became the wealthy 'magnates' of this era. John Brown, Charles Cammell, Thomas Firth, Edward Vickers and Thomas Jessop were perhaps the best known. Tens of thousands of men and women worked round the clock in their huge factories, gargantuan places pouring black smoke, soot and sparks into the air of this broad, once-green valley. Amid all the pollution stood the massed ranks of terraced houses where this workforce lived.

Sheffield became a world leader in metallurgy: Sir Robert Hadfield was the famous pioneer of alloy steels. Harry Brearley invented stainless steel which gave an immediate boost to the local cutlery industry and later to a whole range of modern products still being made in the city.

These great 'east end' firms were kept busy as the British Empire expanded and in the build-up to the Great War. Eventually many of them amalgamated and since the 1960s have been swept away (as modern technology and changing markets brought a revolution) along with those tightly packed areas of outdated housing.

Surprisingly, more steel is produced now in Sheffield than at any previous period – in a few modern, environmentally friendly factories.

RIGHT: *The River Don Engine (1905) powered one of the city's steel-rolling mills. It is one of the world's most powerful steam engines and is still in working order at Kelham Island Industrial Museum.*

ABOVE: *The lower Don Valley between the wars. This landscape, painted from Wincobank by local artist Stanley Royle R.A., gives some idea of the city's heavily industrialized 'east end'.*

RIGHT: *A Bessemer converter, formerly used for making steel, at the entrance to Kelham Island Industrial Museum.*

LEFT: *Bessemer processing in 1895. Detail of painting by W.H. Titcombe.*

A Glimpse of the Past

The Kelham Island Industrial Museum is a remarkable place, an old power station where much of the city's industrial past is brought together. The many exhibits range from locally made vehicles to tradesmen's workshops, gas engines to the mighty River Don steam engine that once powered giant steel-rolling mills.

MADE IN SHEFFIELD

From snuff to sweets to stainless steel

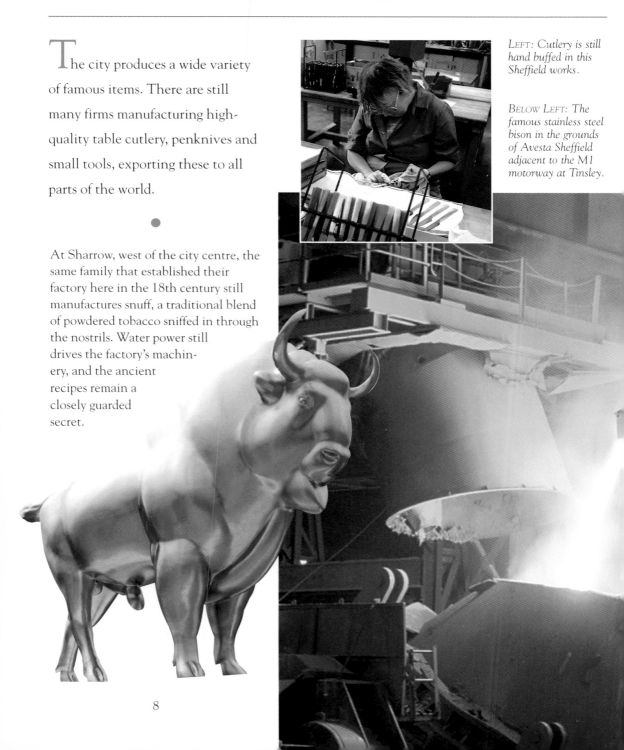

The city produces a wide variety of famous items. There are still many firms manufacturing high-quality table cutlery, penknives and small tools, exporting these to all parts of the world.

●

At Sharrow, west of the city centre, the same family that established their factory here in the 18th century still manufactures snuff, a traditional blend of powdered tobacco sniffed in through the nostrils. Water power still drives the factory's machinery, and the ancient recipes remain a closely guarded secret.

LEFT: Cutlery is still hand buffed in this Sheffield works.

BELOW LEFT: The famous stainless steel bison in the grounds of Avesta Sheffield adjacent to the M1 motorway at Tinsley.

RIGHT: Sheffield's old Canal Wharf has been completely refurbished as Victoria Quays, a popular venue for waterways enthusiasts.

BELOW: Avesta Sheffield is one of the world's largest stainless steel makers.

BELOW RIGHT: Modern Sheffield cutlery continues the area's traditional trade dating from the Middle Ages.

In the north of the city, Trebor Bassett continue to make their world-famous Liquorice Allsorts. George Bassett founded his general confectionery business in 1842. When the firm's only salesman knocked over his tray of samples in front of a customer in 1899, an order was placed – Bassett's Liquorice Allsorts were born. 'Peace Babies' were tiny confections launched by the company to celebrate the end of the First World War. We now know them by the name they were given in 1953, Jelly Babies.

Stainless steel was invented in Sheffield, the first commercial cast being produced in 1913. Avesta Sheffield with its Shepcote Lane factory now has the capacity to produce more than 500,000 tonnes of stainless steel each year – indeed, the company is the largest European and North American supplier of high quality, hot-rolled stainless steel. The city's stainless steel is in great demand to provide the cladding for many of today's most exciting buildings, such as the Canary Wharf Tower and the Lloyd's Building.

THE CITY TODAY

Old splendour and new beginnings

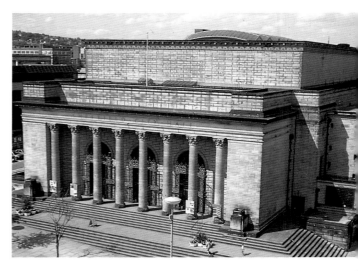

Sheffield became a city in 1893, by which time its population had grown to one third of a million. The Town Hall reflected the newly acquired status. Designed by E.W. Mountford, it is one of the finest Victorian civic buildings in England, and was opened by Her Majesty in person in 1897.

Despite the widespread destruction wrought by the German blitz of 1940, many of Sheffield's best buildings survive, including the neo-Classical City Hall (completed 1934) designed by E. Vincent Harris, with seating for 2,800 people.

The dignified Grecian Cutlers' Hall in Church Street is the third such building to grace this site. It was built in 1832 and extended in 1867. The Company of Cutlers in Hallamshire was founded in 1624 as an organization to protect the interests of the cutlery trade, but from 1860 its remit was extended to include engineering and steel manufacture, too. The famous Cutlers' Feast (or banquet) is held here every September.

The 'Heart of the City' millennium project includes the complete redevelopment of the former Peace Gardens beside the Town Hall and construction of the Winter Gardens on the site of the Town Hall extension.

Not far away, in Norfolk Street, stands the Unitarian Upper Chapel built in 1770. The chapel yard contains sculptures by the local artist George Fullard (1924–73) who rose to fame for his work centred on the anger, suffering and inhumanity of war. The Moor is a long-established pedestrianized thoroughfare with all types of shops, while the Devonshire Quarter is a complex of specialist shops and cafe bars with an alternative shopping centre – The Forum – as its centrepiece.

LEFT: The neo-Classical City Hall was completed in 1934 with seating for 2,800 people.

BELOW LEFT: The statue of the 15th Duke of Norfolk in the Town Hall reminds us that he was Sheffield's first Lord Mayor.

RIGHT: The Town Hall, built 1890–97, was designed by E.W. Mountford and is a fine example of late Victorian municipal architecture.

BELOW: The Cutlers' Feast is held each year in September in the magnificent Cutlers' Hall, Church Street. Founded in 1624, the Company of Cutlers is now associated with all types of steel making and engineering.

BELOW RIGHT: Meadowhall is one of the country's largest out-of-town shopping centres. It occupies the site of a former steel works close to the M1 motorway at Tinsley.

SUPERTRAMS AND SCHOLARSHIPS

Transport and education

It was only in 1819 that Britain's canal system reached the heart of Sheffield's manufacturing district, too late for it to prosper, as the railways arrived less than 20 years later. In 1873, a horse-drawn open tramcar service began, followed by electric trams in 1899. These served the population well until 1960, only to be revived in the form of the city's Supertram network, which opened in 1994.

●

The city has excellent motorway links with the rest of the country: the M1 motorway is only 3 miles (6km) north-east of the centre; the M18 leads east to the A1(M), M180 and both banks of the Humber.

The city's own airport opened at Tinsley in 1998, occupying land reclaimed from industry. It offers links with Amsterdam and other European destinations.

Sheffield has a long and illustrious history of education – boys were being taught grammar and singing by the

monks of Beauchief Abbey as early as 1490. Records tell us that 60 years later church burgesses were paying a schoolmaster in the town. In more recent times several important and successful schools were founded including the Girls' High School, the Convent School of Notre Dame and King Edward VII School for Boys.

ABOVE: Sheffield's Supertrams were introduced in 1994, reflecting the city's fondly remembered earlier electric tramcars.

BELOW: Graduation day at Hallam University.

Sheffield University was created in 1905, its impressive Department of Applied Science following in 1913. Throughout the 20th century it continued to grow, and now has one of the largest student populations in the country. At nearly 80 metres (255 feet), the Arts Tower is the tallest university building in Britain.

Although Sheffield's Hallam University was created from Sheffield Polytechnic as recently as 1992, the Technology and Art Colleges which preceded the 'poly' date back to Victorian times (the School of Art was founded in 1843).

Sheffield College caters for a large number of students over 16. Based on several sites around the city, the college is now the largest further education establishment in Europe.

Looking Around

Firth Court, the original University building of 1905, can be seen at Western Bank near the City Museum and Mappin Art Gallery. The Arts Tower stands nearby.
The Department of Applied Science is in Mappin Street.
Hallam University main buildings stand between the city centre and Midland Railway Station.

ABOVE: *Sheffield University's Firth Court with the Arts Tower behind.*

LEFT: *Rock climbing on Stanage, on the city's western boundary.*

13

Sport and Leisure

National City of Sport

Sheffield has been awarded the accolade of first 'National City of Sport' by the Sports Council because of its wide range of modern facilities. Ponds Forge International Sports Centre in the heart of the city is the best swimming and diving competition venue in Europe.

●

Originally constructed for the 1991 World Student Games, the Don Valley Stadium is destined to become the hub of the country's sporting network with superb training facilities for athletes and a fully-covered all-seater arena – a direct result of Sheffield having been chosen as headquarters of the United Kingdom Sports Institute.

The amateur Sheffield F.C. is reputed to be the world's oldest football club. They now play on a ground near Hillsborough Park. However, their professional neighbours, Sheffield Wednesday, and Bramall Lane counterparts, Sheffield United, excite more attention these days.

Other facilities in and around the city include three municipal golf courses, two outstanding artificial climbing centres and the Sheffield Ski Village, claimed to be Europe's largest all-season ski resort.

The artistic programme on offer is very wide and varied. The restored Lyceum Theatre (1897) presents an outstanding year-round programme of drama, ballet, opera and musicals. Its neighbour, the Crucible Theatre, despite being one of Britain's leading repertory theatres, is perhaps best known for hosting the annual World Professional Snooker Championships.

The Graves Art Gallery, at the Central Library, was built to display paintings bequeathed by the late J.G. Graves, but is also home to the finest collection of Chinese carved ivories in the world – the Grice Collection.

The Mappin Art Gallery (1887) stands next to the City Museum (1937) which houses, among other things, fine cutlery and silver-plate collections. The Ruskin Museum and Craft Gallery celebrate the craftsmanship of the area, also

LEFT: An exciting production at the Crucible Theatre.

BOTTOM LEFT: Sheffield Wednesday play Arsenal at Hillsborough.

containing a selection of Ruskin's own pictures, books and manuscripts. The millennium will see them relocated in a new gallery by the Town Hall.

The spectacularly imaginative National Centre for Popular Music opened in 1999 in the heart of the Cultural Industries Quarter. This is dedicated to the enjoyment of popular music in all its various forms. It provides visitors with the opportunity to experience a unique blend of nostalgic sounds from the past, music from around the world, live performances and insights into how the music business of today really works.

Venues and Teams

Athletics
Don Valley Stadium, Worksop Road, S9 3TL
Basketball
Ponds Forge International Sports Centre,
    Sheaf Street, S1 2BP
Sheffield Arena, Broughton Lane, S9 2DF
    [Sheffield Sharks (men)
    Sheffield Hatters (women)]
Football
Bramall Lane, S2 4SU
    [Sheffield United F.C.]
Hillsborough Stadium, S6 1SW
    [Sheffield Wednesday F.C.]
Ice Hockey
Sheffield Arena, Broughton Lane, S9 2DF
    [Sheffield Steelers]
Rugby League
Don Valley Stadium, Worksop Road, S9 3TL
    [Sheffield Eagles]
Speedway
Owlerton Stadium, Penistone Road S6 2DE
    [Sheffield Tigers]
Swimming
Ponds Forge International Sports Centre,
    Sheaf Street, S1 2BP

Golf Courses
There are three public courses in Sheffield. Visitors can book six days in advance for weekend play or a day in advance for midweek play. There are no membership fees and clubs can be hired.
Beauchief Abbey Lane S8 0BD
Birley Birley Lane S12 3BP
Tinsley High Hazels Park, Darnall S9 4PE

Sheffield Tourist Information Centre also has details of private clubs where golfers who are members of their home clubs can play as guests.

GREEN LUNGS

Parks, open spaces and enchanting relics

Sheffield's magnificent hillsides and valleys, coupled with the long tradition of pride in municipal open spaces, means that the city has over 50 fine public parks. Sheffield contains more woodland than any other English city.

●

The Botanical Gardens, Clarkehouse Road, Broomhall were opened in 1836, containing three large conservatories and a bear pit. Although the last brown bear left in 1870, the pit remains. The conservatories have undergone complete overhaul with the help of a lottery award.

At the top of Meersbrook Park stands one of the city's most interesting buildings. The half-timbered Bishops' House was built in the 16th century and is the best preserved timber-framed house in the Sheffield area, its name commemorating the two sons of William Blythe who became bishops at the turn of the 16th century.

Bishops' House, with its furnished rooms, is one of the city's best museums. Events and activities take place there throughout the year.

Another important historic building in the suburbs is Beauchief Abbey (say bee-chif!), founded in 1183 by monks

of the Premonstratensian Order. What we see today is the lower part of the original tower and a modest church with box pews erected in 1662. The abbey stands in delightful surroundings, protected from development by the Beauchief golf course.

Sheffield's wealth of parks and open spaces, especially to the south, west and

ABOVE: Early summer in Whirlow Brook Park, one of the many public open spaces for which Sheffield is justly renowned.

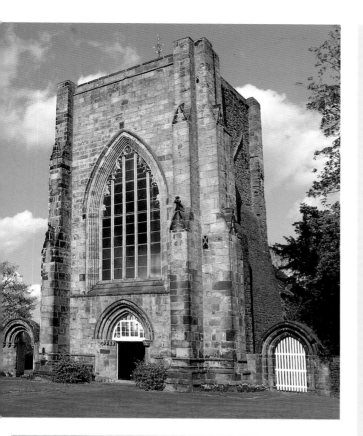

Three Walks

The Sheffield Round Walk

This 10-mile (16km) walk starts at Hunter's Bar, Ecclesall Road, proceeding up the Porter Brook, through the Mayfield Valley to Ringinglow village, then down the Limb Valley to Whirlow and through Ecclesall Wood. The route then passes through escarpment woods to Beauchief Abbey and thence via Graves Park to Norton Church.

There are plenty of public transport services along the route returning to Hunter's Bar.

The Rivelin and Loxley Round Walk

The 9-mile (15km) trail starts and finishes at Malin Bridge, following the banks of the River Rivelin through woods, passing the sites of early water-powered factories, over a ridge and down the Loxley Valley in the north-west of the city.

The Five Weirs Walk

This 5-mile (8km) walk follows the banks of the River Don from close to the city centre down to Meadowhall. A return route via the towpath of the Sheffield and Tinsley Canal provides a most interesting circular urban walk.

There are several good publications giving details of these and other local walks.

ABOVE: *Beauchief Abbey was founded in 1183. It stands surrounded by an attractive public golf course in the south-west of the city.*

LEFT: *Beauchief golf course gives players fine views of the Peak District moors.*

north is unique in Britain. Interesting walking routes link these surprisingly rural spaces. Particularly noteworthy is the 10-mile (16km) Sheffield Round Walk starting at Hunter's Bar and ending at Graves Park. It links various city parks, woodland and historic sites and quickly dispels preconceived ideas any visitor might have about Sheffield as an ugly industrial centre.

THE GOLDEN FRAME

Sheffield's scenic surroundings

The beautiful countryside that girdles much of Sheffield is often called its 'Golden Frame'. The land to the north, west and south is proper hill country – the wildness of some of these areas coming as a real surprise to many visitors.

Sheffield's claim to be Europe's highest industrial city can be appreciated when you realise that the western boundary rises to 546 metres (1,791ft) at Margery Hill.

●

Bradfield Dale is a tilted patchwork of pastures below the frowning moors. A string of reservoirs supplying the city lie along its valley bottom. The parish church of St Nicholas at High Bradfield is one of the finest in South Yorkshire.

Westwards beyond the city boundary lies the Hope Valley, one of the most beautiful areas of the Peak District National Park. Here at Hathersage are connections with the legend of Robin Hood and with Charlotte Bronte's classic *Jane Eyre*.

Towards the head of the Hope Valley lies the Derbyshire village of Castleton, very popular with visitors for Winnats Pass, a limestone gorge, its ruined

ABOVE: *Summer day in Bradfield Dale, looking to High Bradfield village.*

ABOVE: *Haddon Hall, a seat of the Dukes of Rutland, stands above the River Wye near Bakewell. It is one of the county's loveliest old manor houses and is open to the public in summer.*

Norman castle and four excitingly lit show caves where one can descend to see the source of the unique and famous Blue John crystal. To the south-west of Sheffield is the pretty Peak District village of Baslow, near to the world-famous Chatsworth House, seat of the Dukes of Devonshire.

Occupying the lower ground to the east of the city is the Rother Valley Country Park, a landscaped leisure park on the site of reclaimed colliery workings with facilities for sailing, windsurfing, canoeing, jet skis and a cable water-ski tow. Other attractions here include golfing and cycle hire.

ABOVE: One of Castleton's famous crystal caverns.

LEFT: Chatsworth House, seat of the Dukes of Devonshire, lies to the south-west of Sheffield and is one of the most popular of stately homes.

BELOW: Peveril Castle dominates the village of Castleton near the head of the Hope Valley in the Peak District National Park.

Eastern Towns

Rotherham, Barnsley and Doncaster

In medieval times Rotherham, 5 miles (8 kms) to the north-east, was a more important place than Sheffield. The magnificent 15th-century parish church of All Saints confirms this. The Clifton Park Museum, in the 18th-century the house of iron magnate Joshua Walker, contains the country's finest collection of Rockingham porcelain, which was made at nearby Swinton. The restored Catcliffe Glass Kiln was built in 1740 and is the oldest surviving one of its type in western Europe.

●

Barnsley, a dozen miles (19 kms) due north of Sheffield, stands at the edge of wonderful Pennine countryside. The town's huge market was established in 1249; the country house museum of Cannon Hall contains period rooms and decorative arts and stands in a wooded park open to the public.

Doncaster, a Roman settlement and one of England's oldest market towns, is today a busy railway junction, situated on the plain some miles east of Rotherham and Barnsley. The town's architectural pride is the Mansion House, completed in 1748. The impressive parish church (1858) with its 52-metre (170-foot) tower was designed by Sir George Gilbert Scott. The St Leger, the oldest of the five English Classic horse races, was first run at Doncaster in 1776. A flat race of just under two miles, it takes place in the autumn.

Not far from the town are some historic gems: Brodsworth Hall, managed by English Heritage, and Conisbrough Castle, the northern stronghold of the Earls of Surrey, which inspired the famous Sir Walter Scott novel *Ivanhoe*.

ABOVE: Roche Abbey, near Rotherham, was founded by the Cistercians in 1147. Its romantic landscaped ruins are open to the public.

RIGHT: Conisbrough Castle, between the towns of Rotherham and Doncaster, is a dramatic relic of the Norman age It was restored in 1994.